LITTLEHAMPTON
IN OLD PHOTOGRAPHS

SOUTH TERRACE AND COMMON, 1869.

LITTLEHAMPTON
IN OLD PHOTOGRAPHS

COLLECTED BY
IRIS JONES AND
DAPHNE STANFORD

ALAN SUTTON

Alan Sutton Publishing Limited
Phoenix Mill · Far Thrupp · Stroud · Gloucestershire

First Published 1990

British Library Cataloguing in Publication Data

Littlehampton in old photographs.
1. West Sussex. Littlehampton, History
I. Jones, Iris II. Stanford, Daphne
942.267

ISBN 0-86299-718-6

Typeset in 9/10 Korinna.
Typesetting and origination by
Alan Sutton Publishing Limited.
Printed in Great Britain by
Dotesios Printers Limited.

CONTENTS

LITTLEHAMPTON in 1874.

INTRODUCTION

Littlehampton's history goes back to prehistoric times, when people of the Stone and Bronze Ages made their homes here on the east bank of the estuary of the River Arun. A Romano-British settlement later occupied this site.

The arrival of the Normans had a significant effect on the village of Hantone, as it was called in Domesday Book. Roger de Montgomerie took possession of the area and established himself in his castle at Arundel. His successors controlled the development of Littlehampton for hundreds of years afterwards. The Arun became one of the main routes for travellers between England and Normandy, and stone from Caen was a major import here. The main port was at Arundel, although vessels also loaded and unloaded cargoes lower down river, and the whole estuary, then a wide delta, was known as Arundel Haven.

Throughout the Middle Ages the harbour continued to be busy, especially when the Earls of Arundel commanded the English fleets, and its name occasionally appears in history books.

Navigation in the unconfined estuary was always hazardous because of the build-up of sandbanks and shingle, until in 1735 a new channel was cut at the river's outlet, an embankment constructed, and wooden piers erected on both sides of the new river mouth.

The area was a likely landing place for invaders and, in the eighteenth century, a battery on the east bank guarded the harbour entrance, while, in the mid-nineteenth century, a fort was built on the west bank.

In 1801 the population of Littlehampton was 584. During the next thirty years it increased to almost treble that number. Until the late eighteenth century Littlehampton had remained a small village centred around the present High Street. The main occupations of its inhabitants were fishing and agriculture but, as the size of vessels increased, many cargo boats became too large to sail through the narrow stretches of the river to Arundel and used the quays of Littlehampton instead. During the 1830s and 1840s stores and workshops were built here and, early in the nineteenth century, two shipyards were established. In 1869 the port was renamed the Port of Littlehampton and the Customs House was moved here from Arundel.

Between 1863 and 1882 a steam packet service operated to Le Havre, Honfleur and the Channel Islands. Littlehampton had developed into a busy port, and shipping and boat building became its major industries. Ships from here sailed the world, one interesting export being some of the first sheep sent to Australia and the Falkland Islands.

Improvement in the harbour trade coincided with the growing popularity of the seaside holiday. Towards the end of the eighteenth century a hotel opened near the beach, and the Earl of Berkeley chose a site to the east of this for a new house. When the Duke of Norfolk made grants of land to local builders, they began to construct a terrace close to the earl's house.

The new developing area near the sea, built mainly for the benefit of summer visitors, gradually spread westwards. It was separated from the original village by a large expanse of green fields. Even at the end of the nineteenth century Littlehampton consisted of two distinct and very different parts: 'Town', the old village, and 'Beach'. Property owners in the 'Beach' district considered theirs a select area, and among its visiting patrons were members of titled families. 'Town' dwellers looked on the 'Beach' inhabitants as interlopers.

Littlehampton particularly attracted artists and writers, who preferred its relaxed, peaceful atmosphere to the noise and liveliness of larger resorts. Shelley, Coleridge and Cary came here, as well as Byron, who enjoyed swimming in the river. Constable painted the windmill which stood at the river mouth, and the paintings of local scenes by many other artists can be seen in Littlehampton's museum.

The 1860s was a period of great change and increasing prosperity for the town. The population rose by 39 per cent between 1861 and 1871 to 3,272 and confidence in the town's future encouraged the Duke of Norfolk to construct the Esplanade in 1867/8.

The River Arun, however, halted the town's growth in that direction. Expansion was also limited by the fact that most of the land here was the property of one landlord, the Duke of Norfolk. The town benefited, however, from the help given to it by the Norfolk Estate, which bore the expense of making and maintaining the roads, as well as upholding the neatness and cleanliness of the area. The Estate also controlled the town planning, and supported Littlehampton's aim to be a first-class resort.

Efforts to keep the place select were frustrated by the arrival of the railway, and by the 1880s Littlehampton was receiving between two and three thousand visitors a day during the summer season.

The river was not only a barrier to the town's expansion, but also to its communication with other towns. Proposals to build a bridge across the Arun here were opposed by authorities up river and canal companies who feared it would affect their trade. Instead, a chain ferry was brought into use in 1825, and Littlehampton had to wait until 1908 when a swing toll-bridge was opened, a cause for great rejoicing in the town.

The shipbuilding industry declined with the advent of steam vessels, but well-known boat building firms continued to operate here. Part of the river is now a marina, but cargo boats still use the port.

During the late nineteenth century Littlehampton became well established as a holiday resort, patronized mainly by professional people with young families. The flat, sandy beaches and the long, wide stretch of the Green were special attractions; the picturesque harbour, beautiful country walks and easy access to the Downs were additional assets.

In the first half of this century Littlehampton became known as 'The Children's Paradise', a title still appropriate today. The town also had a reputation as a centre for sports, with a nationally known cricket ground, excellent tennis-courts and golf links, fine fishing, as well as boating and sailing facilities. Fresh entertainment for the day-tripper was supplied when the Norfolk Estate sold the windmill site to Billy Butlin who built an amusement park there in 1932.

The post-war years have brought further changes. Littlehampton has continued to expand and is now the headquarters of Arun District Council as well as The Body Shop, founded by Anita Roddick in her home town. Many of the buildings shown in these photographs have disappeared, but some remain to remind us of past Littlehampton.

SECTION ONE

Town

LITTLEHAMPTON HIGH STREET in 1863

HIGH STREET. In the foreground are the pillars fronting Pritchard's the bakers, next door to John White the photographer.

THIS PHOTOGRAPH OF THE HIGH STREET WAS TAKEN shortly before the thatched buildings were demolished to make way for Clifton Road in 1889.

WALTERS AND SIMPSON were fruiterers and fishmongers.

THE CYPRUS TEMPERANCE HOTEL on Island Terrace and, on the left, the future site of the Arcade.

THE HIGH STREET, showing the decorations for the opening of the Swing Bridge. On the right is the frontage of Constable's Anchor Spring Brewery. The tall chimney of the brewery, built in 1871, was a local landmark until removed during the Second World War for security reasons. Brewing had ceased in 1917.

MARTIN'S EAGLE STORES, surmounted by a stone eagle, was pulled down in 1921 to make way for the Arcade.

THIS SITE HAD BEEN OCCUPIED by various grocery stores for more than a century. Previously William Ockenden had established a smithy and ironmongery on part of this site.

SURREY STREET in 1867, showing the Dolphin Hotel at the right-hand end of the road.

A MEWS OFF SURREY STREET in 1936.

SURREY STREET, leading to the River Arun, connects the High Street with the harbour. The post office in the centre of the picture is now the site of the electricity showrooms.

THE GEORGIAN TERRACE IN SURREY STREET in 1910. Isaac's the butchers, later Floyd's Cycle Shop, is next door to Spry the photographer.

DEMOLITION OF BUTT'S ORCHARD WALL in 1912. This had been a hazard to traffic for some years.

WEST END OF HIGH STREET, leading to Terminus Road.

THE BROADWAY DEVELOPMENT being built on the corner of High Street and Surrey Street, with existing shops still trading in front.

TERMINUS ROAD, previously Ferry Road, was renamed when the railway station was relocated from Lyminster. From being a minor access road it became a major route out of town when the bridge was opened in 1908. The creeper-covered house was the home of Robert French, solicitor. Constable's chimney can be seen above the High Street in the distance.

RIVER ROAD. The Ship and Anchor Inn was one of six public houses in the road, which was the industrial centre of the town with wharves, shipbuilding, chandlery shops and engineering workshops. The larger houses in the road were the homes of the shipbuilders and shipowners.

MAUD BURTENSHAW walking down Hampton Court, between Terminus Road and River Road. The cottages, dating from 1796, were demolished in 1950.

HAZELWOOD COTTAGES. This row of typical Sussex seaside flint cottages was demolished in 1937 to make way for Woolworths.

MOST OF THESE HOUSES IN NEW ROAD were built in the 1880s.

CLIFTON ROAD was extended in 1889 to link with the High Street.

VICTORIA TERRACE, said to be Britain's longest unbroken terrace, was built between 1886 and 1888 by Bicknell and Pile, who later became Bicknell and Stone.

BEACH ROAD in the early 1900s. This was the town's smarter shopping street in the 1920s and 1930s.

BEACH ROAD, c. 1930. On the right are the first Council Offices, from 1894 to 1934, opposite Warwick House.

ST CATHERINE'S ROAD has changed little since this photograph was taken, but in 1900 Caffyn's Field was railed and used to graze cattle and horses. The gardeners are cutting Mrs Robinson's hedge, and the horseman is Mr Reeves.

ST CATHERINE'S ROAD, viewed from the south. The common extended to this point before Irvine Road was built up.

A WINTRY SCENE IN FITZALAN ROAD in 1904. The name marks the town's close association with the Duke of Norfolk's family.

THE MANOR HOUSE, an old farmhouse dating from about 1830, was converted to Council Offices in 1933. The town pump was removed in 1932.

THESE EARLY NINETEENTH-CENTURY BUILDINGS on Island Terrace stood beside the village pond. The office of the Local Board of Health was nearer East Street.

HAMPTON COTTAGE in East Street, one of the town's older houses, was formerly part of a farmhouse. At the time of this photograph it was a tea-room.

CHURCH STREET. The Olympic Hall, on the left, was a theatre and roller-skating rink before becoming the Palladium Cinema.

A NOSTALGIC RURAL SCENE. These Church Street cottages were demolished for road widening.

Church Street, Littlehampton.

THE CARRIAGE is turning into the gate of the old vicarage in Church Street.

THE OLD MAIN ROAD TO WORTHING. In 1900 East Street was a quiet lane.

HELYER'S FARM IN EAST STREET, looking much as it does today. Part of it dates back to 1710.

STEPHEN OLLIVER'S NEW HOUSE at the end of East Street in the 1890s.

DUKE STREET'S FLINT COTTAGES were built of sea-cobbles in 1832. Several were demolished for a car park, but the rest, and the Globe Inn, still remain.

A PEACEFUL AND ALMOST DESERTED ARUNDEL ROAD, looking south, in 1900, showing the spacious villas built by Robert Bushby at the southern end of the street. Bushby (1813–91) was a local builder responsible for many of the buildings in the area from about 1840.

MOLLIE GREY'S COTTAGE at the bend in Arundel Road, demolished in 1905 when Clun Road was constructed.

A SHADY TREE-LINED ROAD TO WICK from Littlehampton.

MAURICE OCKENDEN AND HIS DAUGHTER drive down Wick Street from their home, in 1895.

EVEN IN THE 1930s WICK STREET was often empty of traffic.

THE HAMLET OF TODDINGTON is about a mile from Littlehampton. The farmhouse is a listed building, dating from the late sixteenth century.

HOLLY ACRE FARMHOUSE, now demolished, also in Toddington Lane.

JASMINE AND VIRGINIA COTTAGES in Toddington Lane.

A PANORAMIC VIEW FROM THE CHURCH TOWER, looking seawards. Note the dilapidated mill in the distance, the war memorial behind the trees in the centre, and the Council Offices in the foreground. The photograph would appear to have been taken in the late 1920s, after the street lighting had been converted to electricity.

SECTION TWO

Beach

AN IMPORTANT INGREDIENT of a seaside holiday.

THE RESIDENTIAL NORTHERN END OF NORFOLK ROAD in 1912. Some of these large houses were built by Bushby.

THE OLDER SOUTHERN END OF NORFOLK ROAD is part of the shopping area. It still has the atmosphere of a village street.

THE EASTERN END OF WESTERN ROAD contains some of the oldest houses in the town. The sign of the New Inn Mews is visible on the site of Harris's Riding School.

HARRIS'S RIDING SCHOOL AND STABLES in 1923.

THE WEST END OF WESTERN ROAD. Built in the late 1850s, many of these buildings were lodging houses at this time.

TWENTY YEARS LATER, several had been converted into shops and this had become a busy shopping area. The buildings have now reverted to dwellings.

SELBORNE PLACE, built by Bushby in 1869 and originally part of Western Road.

THE SAME TERRACE approximately sixty years later, and very much the same today.

THE TENNIS GROUND in 1890. In 1881 Robert Bushby's plans to build on this open space, opposite the Beach Hotel, were turned down. Blocks of flats were built here over eighty years later.

A CLOSE UP OF GRANVILLE TERRACE, built C. 1888 by Bushby.

SURREY HOUSE, built for the Earl of Berkeley, was acquired by the Earl of Surrey, became a boys' boarding school, a hotel and then a private house.

BUILT BETWEEN 1803 and 1820, the varying styles of the first section of South Terrace are the work of different builders.

A CHARMING ENGRAVING OF ORIELTON PLACE in 1869. This continuation of South Terrace, built by Bushby, extended from Norfolk Road to St Augustine Terrace.

ANOTHER PART OF SOUTH TERRACE, named after the daughter of Henry I who landed at Littlehampton on her journey to claim the throne of England. Empress Maud Road ran from Granville Terrace to Pier Road.

THE DRINKING FOUNTAIN ON THE GREEN. Long disappeared but remembered with affection by former Littlehampton children and visitors.

LITTLEHAMPTON'S LONG AND SANDY BEACH has been a favourite playground for generations of holiday-makers.

A CROWDED BEACH AND PROMENADE on a breezy summer's day around 1900.

The Parade, Littlehampton

THE SAME EASTWARD VIEW at a quieter period of the year, taken later this century.

HOLIDAY-MAKERS STROLLING WESTWARDS towards the River Arun.

THE PROMENADE PIER was formed when the old east jetty was improved in 1873.

THE UNSPOILT, SANDY WEST BEACH, now sheltered by dunes, has always been popular with those seeking a more secluded bathing place: it ends at Clymping Mill.

CLYMPING MILL, which dates back to 1799, is now a school.

AN ATTRACTIVE VIEW FROM THE JETTY. The wooden lighthouse, demolished during the Second World War, was replaced by a modern concrete one in 1945.

A PEACEFUL CORNER OF THE COMMON. South Terrace is seen across the ornamental lake.

THE OYSTER POND was made in the late eighteenth century, when the oyster trade flourished, to store the oysters brought ashore from the oyster beds. In 1895 it was turned into an ornamental lake. The Arun Mill was built in 1831 to replace an earlier one. The mill ceased functioning in 1913 and lay in ruins until demolished by Butlin in 1932 to make way for an amusement park.

A RIVERSIDE PARADE was first considered in 1873, and eventually planned in 1914 but, delayed by the outbreak of war, it was not finally constructed until 1929/30.

THE CONSTRUCTION OF THE RIVERSIDE PARADE seen from across the river.

A VIEW OF PIER ROAD from the west bank of the Arun.

PIER ROAD looking south, showing the *Worthing Belle* and the windmill.

ORIGINALLY CALLED HENLEY'S BUILDINGS, this row of houses was built in 1829/30. The terrace, at one time Muscle Row, perhaps on account of the muscular occupants, was later Mussel Row, possibly because of their trade. The houses were rebuilt in 1929.

River

RIVER AND OYSTER POND.

A PICTURESQUE SCENE. Fishermen and lobster-pots with sailing ships anchored in the harbour.

THE VIEW DOWNRIVER in the 1930s, showing David Hillyard's well-known boat-building firm.

A VIEW OF THE MOUTH OF THE RIVER showing both navigational lights and the windmill. The *Trina Cecilie* is leaving the harbour under sail, having had a full refit in Harvey's yard. This photograph by Spry is one of a series he took during the course of the refit, all of which he published as postcards.

THE OLD PADDLE TUG *Jumna* began work in the harbour in 1884. Used to tow sailing ships in and out of the river, she was eventually sold to a London firm of contractors and ended her days in Iraq. The name has been perpetuated in the present harbour master's boat.

A QUIET CORNER OF THE HARBOUR.

THE HARBOUR, looking north, showing a variety of craft using the river.

SECTION FOUR

Transport

THE OLD CHAIN FERRY.

THE CHAIN FERRY, built by Thomas Isemonger in 1825, was originally wooden, but replaced by an iron pontoon in 1870. It was the length and width of a carriage and four horses. The Steam Packet Hotel, on the north bank, was so named after the cross-Channel steamers which plied between Littlehampton and Honfleur, via Le Havre and the Channel Islands, during the nineteenth century, before Newhaven was developed as a port.

OLD FERRY, NEW BRIDGE!

THE NEW SWING BRIDGE, constructed in 1908, was replaced by a footbridge in 1981 after a new road bridge had been opened further up river.

THE *EBENEZER*, passing through the new bridge in 1908. Owned by the Robinsons, *Ebenezer* was the last of their sailing fleet and sank near Belfast in 1914.

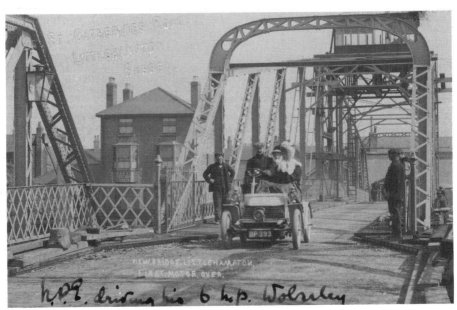

NEVILLE PERRIN EDWARDS driving the first motor car across the bridge, before the official opening.

MISS PANNELL outside Spry's Photographic Studio in Surrey Street.

NORRIS'S MOTOR BUS AND CREW in Fitzalan Road. This firm was later sold to the Southdown Motor Company.

HARRIS'S ONE-HORSE BUS outside the railway station used to transport visitors and their luggage to the 'Beach'.

NOT EVERY TOWN has its own railway engine. This was the last of the class to be built. Very appropriate as Littlehampton is the end of the line!

STROUDLEY A/AIX 80/680 of the London, Brighton and South Coast Railway, and its crew, at Littlehampton station. Gloucester Road is in the background.

ENGINES NOS. 158 AND 294 entering the engine shed at Littlehampton. The engine shed is a listed building so it is still standing, with a brand new station built around it. The former police station is behind No. 158.

SECTION FIVE

Industry

ARUN WINDMILL.

UNLOADING TIMBER AT THE BALTIC WHARF for John Eede Butt in 1925. The majority of the timber came from Riga, in Latvia.

THIS PHOTOGRAPH, by Russell of Chichester, shows John Eede Butt's timber-yard, established around 1820. Butt's had the first telephone in Littlehampton, which was used for playing matches between Brighton and Chichester Chess Clubs.

THE NORFOLK STEAM SAW MILL at John Eede Butt's was installed in 1870, when the tall chimney, a local landmark, was built. This was partly demolished in 1940 and finally removed in the 1970s. The picture shows the steam-powered saw.

WORKMEN ENGAGED IN CONSTRUCTING THE WORTHING ROAD in Wick, during 1928.

BRICKMAKING. There were four main brickfields here, all in the north of the town.

DUKE AND OCKENDEN'S PREMISES in Terminus Road. They were water engineers and well borers from the 1860s.

BUILT FOR THE CROSS-CHANNEL STEAM PACKET in the 1860s, the Railway Wharf was later used for unloading coal, much of it for the Gas Company.

THE PICTURE SHOWS *The Britannia* in Harvey's shipyard. The patent slipway was installed for repair work by Stephen Olliver. Henry Harvey of Rye, a master shipbuilder, took over and built up the yard which remained in the Harvey family for over seventy years.

THE KETCH *Ena*, owned by Joseph Robinson, at Littlehampton in 1906, with Harvey's shipyard in the background. The Robinson brothers, Joseph and George, both master mariners, set up a shipping business in the mid-nineteenth century and their fleet of ships sailed the world.

ONE OF A SERIES OF PHOTOGRAPHS showing the launch of the barge *Wessex* from Harvey's yard c. 1915. An earlier vessel built in this yard, the barque *Trossachs*, took the first sheep and shepherds to the Falkland Islands on her maiden voyage. Her master was Captain Butcher of Arundel.

FISHING BOATS moored at the hard in Pier Road. St John's church is left of centre in the background. Known as the 'fishermen's church', it was built in 1877, founded by a group which left the parish church in protest at High Church practices. It later became a theatre when the congregation moved to St James's.

FISHERMAN DARKIE THOMPSON on his boat with two friends, repairing their nets. Darkie was one of the best known fishermen of the south coast and coxswain of the lifeboat.

CREW OF THE BARQUE *Atossa* of Littlehampton (master, Joseph Robinson) photographed in Atlantic Basin, Brooklyn, New York in May 1888.

WORKMEN AT CONSTABLE'S BREWERY, photographed in the brewery yard.

IN CONTRAST, THE STAFF OF CLARK AND ROBINSON, ironmongers and cycle repairers pose in the studio in their Sunday best.

SECTION SIX

Trade

OLLIVER'S WICK FARM MILK FLOAT.

BANFIELD'S, POULTERER'S, C. 1885, stood here in the High Street until the late 1880s, when new shops were built.

GROOM'S STORES FACED SURREY STREET. George Groom bought the store from Peter Ellison when he came to the town from Suffolk in 1892. The town's first telephone exchange was on the first floor. The shop later became the Forrest Stores and the site is now occupied by a Gateway supermarket.

THE OLDEST SURVIVING BUILDING IN THE HIGH STREET. Built in the eighteenth century, it was formerly known as Carrey's Corner. Neville Smart's Drug Store was a general shop before becoming a pharmacy. A man of all trades, Neville Smart opened the business in 1836. With no qualifications he acted as chemist, dentist, vet, postmaster, printer, newsagent, wine merchant, tobacconist, watchmaker and jeweller. He died in 1882.

H. BURTON AND SONS, 5a High Street, c. 1912. The meat was unprotected from the dust and dirt of the street.

SPARKS were for many years estate agents, auctioneers and furniture makers in the High Street. These premises now house the Gas Company and a travel agent.

A VIEW OF THE HIGH STREET, taken during the early 1920s by Littlehampton photographer Spry. It shows the Crown Hotel before the external alterations, and the Forrest Stores. On the southern side of the street is A. Cowles, drapers, Sparks, and Mann's Drapery Stores.

SURREY STREET, showing Norris the grocers, and the larger premises of Harris, saddlers and harness-makers. Beyond is a small shop fronted by a large royal coat of arms, remaining from the days when the building was occupied by William Dyer, tailor, who retired in 1865.

THE SHOPS SHOWN IN THIS PART OF NORFOLK ROAD are, nearest the camera, William Latter, butcher, the sub post office of Edwin Baker and, in the centre of the picture, the dairy of Richard and Christopher Cobden. These shops were interspersed with apartments for the holiday trade.

MAYS' STATIONERS AND LENDING LIBRARY at the corner of the High Street and Beach Road. Olive Glanville, on the extreme right, was one of what would appear to be an all female staff.

THIS OLD SHOP on the corner of Surrey Street has been used by many trades. Now a hairdressers, it retains its unusual curved door.

THE HORSE-DRAWN OIL TANKER of the Anglo-American Oil Co. pictured near their oil depot in River Road in 1900.

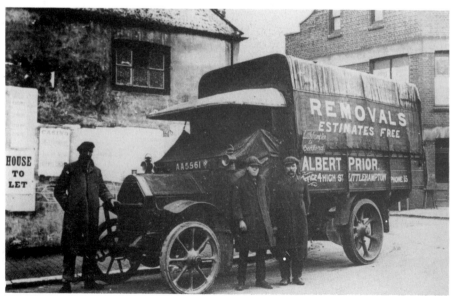

ALBERT PRIOR'S REMOVAL VAN in Clifton Road in the early 1920s.

SECTION SEVEN

Services

THE WATER-TOWER IN ST FLORA'S ROAD.

PARADING THE *BROTHERS FREEMAN* LIFEBOAT through the streets when it came to the town in 1904. This custom had started in 1884 and continued every year on Lifeboat Day. The lifeboat had been provided out of a legacy to the RNLI by Mr Frances J. Freeman.

LAUNCHING THE LIFEBOAT FROM PIER ROAD. The *Brothers Freeman* was a self-righting, 10-oar rowing-boat, 35 ft long and 8 ft wide, and was stationed at Littlehampton till 1922. Littlehampton was then without a lifeboat until *Blue Peter 1* inshore lifeboat arrived in 1967.

AN EARLY LIFEBOAT CREW. Unfortunately, no record remains of their names.

COASTGUARD COTTAGES, built between 1843 and 1850 to house the men who were not allowed to serve in their own home area.

THE FIRE-ENGINE, pictured in Surrey Street in 1927 with an enthusiastic crew. Standing on the running-board is Mr Chatsfield.

THE PART-TIME FIRE-FIGHTERS WITH THEIR ENGINE. Mr Bransbery, Officer in Charge, seated beside the driver, was landlord of The Cow public house.

LAYING THE WATER MAIN TO WICK in 1898 was a task requiring a large number of men before mechanization.

Schools and Churches

THE OLD LITTLEHAMPTON CHURCH, demolished in 1824.

MISS BONIFACE AND THE GIRLS OF EAST STREET SCHOOL. A native of the town, Miss Boniface spent her life teaching in this school and became its headmistress.

THE SCHOOL WAS OPENED in 1878 as a Board School and later became East Street Girls' School. It is now the Flintstone Centre.

AN UNUSUAL VIEW OF THE PLAYGROUND of East Street School before the building of Goda Road.

LYMINSTER SCHOOL in Wick Street opened in 1879 and is still in use today.

ST MARY'S, built in 1824–6 and demolished in 1933, incorporated the original fourteenth-century window, also in the present church.

ROMAN CATHOLIC ST CATHERINE'S was built in 1863 on land donated by the Duke of Norfolk.

THE CONGREGATIONAL CHURCH, built in 1860/1 by Robert Bushby. The steeple was blown down in a gale in 1866, damaging the roof.

THE WESLEYAN METHODIST CHURCH in New Road was built as St Saviour's in 1877. Before becoming the Methodist church it had been a theatre.

SECTION NINE

Sport and Leisure

A LITTLEHAMPTON-BUILT PLEASURE BOAT, *Prince Eddie.*

BEACH HOTEL TENNIS GROUNDS. Contests held here attracted large crowds and play was often of a high standard.

LITTLEHAMPTON TENNIS CLUB in 1909. Mr Teunon, the chemist, is seated on the grass on the right.

LITTLEHAMPTON FOOTBALL TEAM 1895/6. Front row, left to right: J. Piper, T. Newell, R. Wadham, R. Hale, W. Cobby. Second row: W. Sewell, M. Ide, J. Langrish, W. Wilson. Third row: ? Taverner, J. Handscombe. G.R. Redman is on the far left and P. Briggs on the right.

LITTLEHAMPTON has not had a rugby XV since before the Second World War.

THE ATHLETIC CLUB MEETINGS drew entries from all over the country. Meetings were Gala Days with thousands of spectators. Club trainer, Mr Stanyon, is on the left.

LADIES' GOLF TOURNAMENT in 1912. The Golf Club was founded in 1889 on the west bank of the River Arun, near the West Beach. Some of the hats would appear to be more hindrance than help.

THE SAILING CLUB. Commodore Maurice Ockenden is seated fourth from left. Mr Healey, seated second from left, hired out boats on the river.

FIRE BRIGADE SPORTS in 1906. A reminder of the days when raising the funds for the fire brigade was the responsibility of the townspeople.

A CRICKET CLUB HAS EXISTED IN THE TOWN since 1851. This team, photographed during Visitors' Week, 1907, includes B.J. Constable, A.W. Fitzroy Somerset, R.F. Mitchell and H. Mitchell.

CONNAUGHT BOWLING CLUB, c. 1900. The site of this, the first bowling club in Littlehampton, now lies under the surface of Franciscan Way.

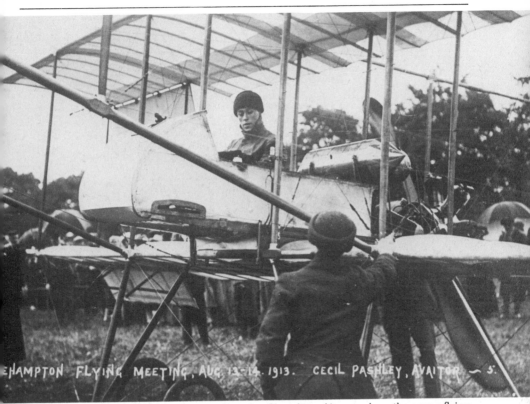

HAMPTON FLYING MEETING, AUG. 13-14. 1913. CECIL PASHLEY, AVAITOR ~ 5.

CECIL PASHLEY AND HIS BROTHER, ERIC, were based at Shoreham Airport, where they ran a flying school. The aircraft was a Henri Farman biplane. Some meetings of the local flying club took place in Littlehampton. There are still pilots flying today who were taught by Cecil Pashley.

PHYSICAL FITNESS was very much in vogue in the 1930s. *The Daily Express* arranged keep-fit classes, on the common at high tide and on the sands at low tide, during the summer months.

Under the Patronage of

Mr. John Oliver.

On FRIDAY EVENING, JUNE 3rd, 1825,

His Majesty's Servants will act the Musical Drama of

TURN OUT

Or, the Mad Politician.

Forge......Mr. CHAPLIN	Gregory Redtail.........Mr. BURTON		
Doctor Truckle.....Mr. MILLAR	Reeve.......Mr. OSBORNE		
Mr Ramsey......Mr. CLARK	William.............Mr. JONES		
Somerville........Mr. BOOTH	James...........Mr. DAVIES		
Marian Ramsey................Mrs. BOOTH			

End of the Drama,

A COMIC SONG BY MR. MILLER.

After which, the favourite Entertainment of The

CHILDREN in the WOOD

Sir Rowland.....Mr. MILLER	Lord Alford.........Mr. BOOTH	
Oliver......Mr. CLARK	Apathy.......Mr. OSBORNE	
Gabriel......Mr BURTON	Ruffian...........Mr. JONES	
Walter.....(the Carpenter).....Mr. CHAPLIN		
The Children......Master and Miss CHAPLIN		
Josephine ....Mrs. BOOTH		

A Popular Song by Mr. Booth.

A DANCE BY MISS CHAPLIN.

A New Comic Song by Mr. Osborne.

The whole to conclude with the popular Farce, of The

SPECTRE BRIDEGROOM

Or, A Ghost in Spite of Himself.

The Characters by Mr. CHAPLIN. Mr. BURTON. Mr. OSBORNE. Mr. BOOTH.
Mr. CLARK. Mr. JONES. Mrs. BOOTH. and Mrs. CHAPLIN.

Tickets and Places for the Boxes to be taken daily, of Mr. Chaplin, at Capt. Mark Carpenter's, Sea Craught.
The remainder of the Nights of Performance will be on Mondays, Wednesdays, & Fridays

W. CLEMENTS, PRINTER, WORTHING.

THE NEW THEATRE was a converted barn which stood in the High Street, opposite the Congregational Church. It opened in 1807, was lit by gas from the summer of 1848, and was demolished in the late 1890s.

SANGER'S CIRCUS, seen parading through the town in 1886, brought crowds of sightseers.

THE CARNIVAL is a lively annual event, only interrupted by the war years. It is here photographed by John White, from the window above his studio.

THE COMMON has always been an asset to the town. Its wide open expanse has been a safe, inviting leisure area for visitors and townsfolk for both formal and informal activities.

HARRY JOSEPH started entertaining audiences in Littlehampton in 1892. During the following winter he held theatrical performances in the Victoria Hall, New Road, formerly St Saviour's church. In the summer he staged pierrot shows on the Green, with his own troupe. In 1912 he opened his Kursaal, a combined pierrot theatre and fun palace, next to Arun Mill.

THE DECK-CHAIR AUDIENCE at Harry Joseph's benefit on 19 August 1908. Master Robinson is in the front row, wearing a cap.

HARRY JOSEPH'S PIERROT TROUPE in front of the Beach Hotel wall.

Bandstand and Shelter Hall, Littlehampton.

A VIEW OF THE BANDSTAND, showing the mill and the Western Shelter Pavilion, which was given to the town by the Duke of Norfolk.

THE BANDSTAND was a popular venue for open-air concerts.

The Bandstand, Littlehampton

BANJO ROAD was laid out on the Green in 1905. The Pavilion was built in 1924.

THE COMMON AND AMUSEMENT PARK, LITTLEHAMPTON

THE NORFOLK ESTATES sold the windmill site to Billy Butlin in 1932. The old mill and Kursaal were demolished and the fun-fair built there.

THE SWIMMING POOL opened on the beach opposite Norfolk Road in 1919 but had a short life and closed in May 1934.

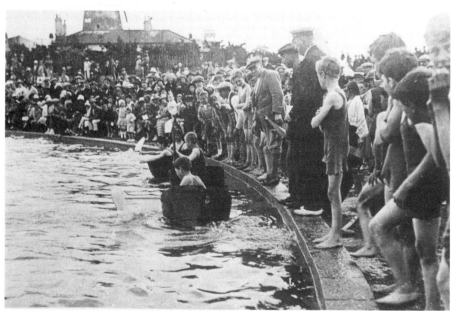

LOCAL WATERMEN ORGANIZED AN ANNUAL REGATTA for children on the Oyster Pond; an afternoon of fun and entertainment.

THE FAIR CAME TO LITTLEHAMPTON on 26 May each year, and was held along Surrey Street and on to Fisherman's Hard. Said to be one of the oldest charter fairs in the area, stall holders were not allowed to claim their pitch before six o'clock the previous evening. This led to a frantic scramble on the stroke of six. On the Fisherman's Hard the row of swingboats was so placed that they swung out over the river. Traffic problems led to its removal in 1933 to Linden Park.

OUTDOOR WHIST DRIVES were the fashion in the 1920s. This one was held in the Manor House, the home of Mrs Drummond-Murray who is seated in the foreground.

A SMART TURN-OUT OF LITTLEHAMPTON YOUTH.

THE WHITTLE FAMILY, photographed at Toddington Tea Gardens, a favourite summer venue for Littlehampton residents. This tea party took place in 1911, when Mr Whittle came home from Egypt. The Tea Gardens, run by the Corney family, were a pleasant rural stroll across the fields.

THE OLD MUSEUM occupied the rear room of the library, the entrance guarded by an enormous, stuffed grizzly bear. In 1965 the need for extra space for books led to the museum being closed. A large proportion of the contents were sold and the museum moved to River Road. The fate of the rather moth-eaten bear is unknown.

THE BEACH HOTEL was built around 1775. Dances and other social functions were held in the adjoining Assembly Rooms.

A NEW HOTEL was built alongside the old buildings in 1887.

BUILT BEFORE 1824, the Norfolk was a major hotel in the town.

THE NORFOLK was a stopping point for the stagecoach from London.

BY THE TIME THIS PHOTOGRAPH WAS TAKEN, around 1912, the façade of the Norfolk Hotel had been given bay windows and a more impressive entrance. The hotel was closed in 1958 and demolished in 1959. Further along the street is the Dolphin Hotel, dating from 1784, where Lord Byron once stayed.

THE WHITE HART was originally The Swan, then The Dolphin. The coach is thought to have been on a commemorative run of the Brighton to Portsmouth stage.

THE GEORGE INN transferred to Arundel Road from the High Street in the 1820s, where it was run as a posting house.

THE COW public house in East Street, before being rebuilt in the 1930s.

FORMERLY TWO ESTABLISHMENTS, the Nelson and Victory, dating from the early nineteenth century, gave its name to the nearby landing stage, the Nelson Steps.

THE NEW INN a family hotel and posting house since 1819.

THE PRINCE OF WALES in Western Road was here by 1882. It was the winning-post for the horse races once held on the common. No longer a public house, it is nowadays a hairdressers's salon.

Events and Disasters

A VIEW OF THE FAIR.

THIS PHOTOGRAPH, taken by John White, shows the Jubilee Arch, erected in the High Street to celebrate the Golden Jubilee of Queen Victoria in 1887. The building on the right with rounded windows is now Ockenden's, ironmongers.

THE PROCESSION FOR THE GOLDEN JUBILEE setting off from outside the railway station.

LORD EDMUND TALBOT, MP, laying the foundation stone of Littlehampton Public Library in 1905. The first in West Sussex, it was financed by the Carnegie Foundation.

IN 1897 A FUND WAS STARTED to celebrate Queen Victoria's Diamond Jubilee. By 1904 enough money had been raised to provide a hospital for the town. No. 18 Surrey Street, the town's first post office, was chosen, despite requiring considerable repair and alteration. Opened by the Duke of Norfolk, the hospital had a medical staff of six and a dentist.

EMPIRE DAY AT LYMINSTER SCHOOL in 1909. A special day for schools throughout the British Empire, chosen to celebrate Queen Victoria's birthday on 24 May. The day was established to promote the teaching of 'Citizenship and Empire Knowledge'.

CAREFULLY POSED FOR THE CAMERA are some of the men who built the bridge, with the first horses to cross.

THE OPENING OF THE BRIDGE was an occasion for great celebrations in the town. Here the pupils of Lyminster School are seen marching down Wick Street to attend the ceremony, which was followed by a Grand Tea Party on Rope Walk for all the schoolchildren, and then sports.

THE EXPECTANT CROWD IN TERMINUS ROAD, waiting for the Duke of Norfolk to arrive to open the Swing Bridge. Littlehampton's motto is prominently displayed on the banner. Outside Littlehampton enthusiasm for the bridge was lukewarm. Without the driving power of three men, Neville Perrin Edwards, George Groom and the Revd Henry Green, the bridge may not have been built.

HIS GRACE THE DUKE OF NORFOLK opened the bridge, the ceremony being attended by civic dignitaries from across the county, on a beautifully sunny 27 May 1908. That night the bridge was decorated with fairy lights, courtesy of the Littlehampton Gas Company.

THE OLD CHAIN FERRY LEAVING THE TOWN. It was bought by S. Ockenden and converted into a houseboat, finishing its life on the River Hamble.

THE ST JOHN AMBULANCE BRIGADE parading through the town to display their new 'Walking Ambulance' in 1911.

JOSE WEISS, AN AVIATION PIONEER, experimented with gliders, making trial flights from Amberley Mount in June 1909. He later advanced to powered flight and in April 1910 he tested his monoplane on Clymping Sands. After take-off his machine overturned, throwing out the pilot, Gerald Leake, who was unhurt. Weiss was a prolific artist who sold many of his 2,500 paintings to finance his aeronautical experiments.

LADY PERCY ST MAUR, of Surrey House, laying the foundation stone of the new hospital in Fitzalan Road in 1911.

LADY HENRY FLETCHER OPENING THE HOSPITAL in 1912. The tall gentleman with the white beard is Mr William Beldam.

CAPTURED GERMAN GUNS ON RAILWAY WHARF in 1918.

THE 'PEACE PROCESSION' IN SURRY STREET in 1919, photographed from the first-floor window of the Forrest Stores, by Spry.

CROWDS ASSEMBLED AT THE OPENING CEREMONY when the Littlehampton Urban District Council moved to the Manor House in 1934. The opening was performed by two local school-children, Joan Strong and Eric Laker.

A FIRE IN SURREY STREET on 17 December 1868 destroyed a row of cottages and shops. Woolworths' store now occupies the site.

FIRE AT THE ELECTRIC PALACE in 1922. Previously the Terminus Theatre and Skating Rink, it became the Regent Cinema in 1931.

THE PAVILION, a wooden building, was destroyed by fire in July 1928, quickly rebuilt, and opened in August of the same year.

LIKE ALL SEASIDE RESORTS, Littlehampton has suffered from gale damage over the years.

PARTS OF LITTLEHAMPTON WERE FREQUENTLY FLOODED. This picture of River Road shows Mr Ockenden in the doorway, Captain Scarpe pretending to fish, and boys delivering post by *Duckling* in 1908.

PIER ROAD was another area liable to flood, as shown in this photograph of 1932.

EAST STREET was also prone to flooding, especially in the vicinity of the bus station.

THE SCENE ON THE GOLF LINKS when the River Arun burst its banks in 1913.

THE BARQUE *Glitza* aground and overturned at Railway Wharf. Joseph Robinson wired the owner and bought her for £80.

A STEAMROLLER brought low by a hole in the road.

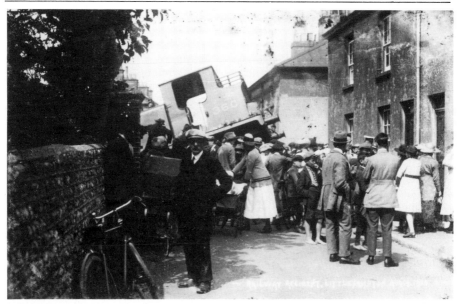

LITTLEHAMPTON'S BEST-REMEMBERED PRE-WAR DISASTER.

THESE ARE JUST TWO OF MANY PHOTOGRAPHS taken when engine No. 360 reversed through the buffers and then the wall into Albert Road.

SECTION ELEVEN

People

MOLLIE GREY, SWEETMAKER.

ALBION OCKENDEN with his second wife, Caroline, and thirteen of his seventeen children. The fourteenth, Maurice, was buying wood in Sweden when this photograph was taken. In later years members of the family emigrated to Canada, America, Australia and New Zealand. In recent years their descendants have travelled back to Littlehampton to discover their roots.

JOHN HARVEY, JP, son of Henry Harvey, on Littlehampton Bridge with a guard, during the First World War. John, owner of the shipyard, was a public benefactor and supporter of the Congregational Church. He ran the family yard for nearly fifty years.

GEORGE GROOM, GROCER had five stores in the town. He became chairman of the UDC and was one of the chief campaigners for the bridge.

DR CECIL LAST came to Littlehampton in 1902 and served in the hospital from 1911 to 1939. He was the first president of the Littlehampton Rotarians, and the police surgeon.

A HARBOUR COMMISSION was first appointed in the 1730s to improve the condition of the river, then almost blocked by sand spits. Here some of the commissioners are making their annual tour of inspection, a day when ships were dressed overall and which ended, for the commissioners, with the Asparagas Feast at the New Inn. In the boat are the harbour master in the bows and, among the commissioners, Captain Mostyn, agent to the Duke of Norfolk in the shiny top hat, George Sparks, Richard Holmes and his son, Captain Hills, RN, and George Butt, with boatmen Collins, Churchill and Miles.

ALF 'BADGER' BOWLEY, a local fisherman, pictured in the 1920s.

SIR HUBERT PARRY on board *Wanderer*, an old
east coast trawler converted by Harvey's for
Sir Hubert. The famous composer lived at
Rustington.

THE SHORTEST ROUTE from the town to the club room and the first tee of the golf course was by ferry. Many famous golfers used the Littlehampton Ferry, a small rowing-boat. Best remembered today as the founder of the British Legion Poppy Day Appeal Fund, Field Marshal Earl Haig is here pictured on his way to the links.

INTERNATIONALLY FAMOUS Scottish music-hall entertainer, Sir Harry Lauder, fourth from left, was a very keen golfer who described his hobby as 'trying to hit a wee gutty ba' '.

ALBERT, DUKE OF YORK, later King George VI, waiting on the ferry steps, after playing golf at Littlehampton Golf Club in the late 1920s. His brother, the Prince of Wales, also enjoyed visiting this course.

JOSEPH ROBINSON, shipowner, master mariner, member of the Local Board of Health and Littlehampton Urban District Council, pictured in his garden at the age of eighty-eight years in 1908.

ACKNOWLEDGEMENTS

We would like to express our gratitude to the following for lending photographs or giving information:

Val and Tony Chapman • Peter Cheney • Phyllis Cowles • Joyce Cunningham Winifred Diprose • Sydney Fogg • Tyndall Jones • Joan Last and Herbert Whittle.

We are especially grateful to Carolyn Brown and Oliver Gilkes of Littlehampton Museum for all their assistance and generous help.